# THE COTSWOLDS
## IN COLOUR

# THE
# COTSWOLDS
# IN COLOUR

*A Collection of Colour Photographs*

*With an Introductory Text
and Notes on the Illustrations by*
JOHN BLEDLOW

LONDON
B. T. BATSFORD LTD

*First Published 1957*

PRINTED AND BOUND IN GREAT BRITAIN
BY W. S. COWELL LTD, LONDON AND IPSWICH
FOR THE PUBLISHERS
**B. T. BATSFORD LTD**
4 FITZHARDINGE STREET, PORTMAN SQUARE, LONDON, W.1

# CONTENTS

# LIST OF ILLUSTRATIONS

# I  COTSWOLD REVISITED

WHEN I planned to refresh my memory of the Cotswolds by doing a point-to-point round of them on my bicycle I did not feel at all optimistic about the adventure. That there would be a vast number of hills to walk up was an inescapable fact, and it seemed most likely that the weather as well as gravity would be against me. February had reserved its rain, March had come in like a lamb: now it was nearly the end of April and still the lion had not put in an appearance and was likely to come roaring at any moment in company with a delayed-action Filldyke.

In the event, I was wrong in all these forebodings. The weather was perfect, the countryside so beautiful, and the hedgerows so rich with new greenery and spring flowers that going slow on foot up hill was no penalty: Except for the Easter week-end, the tourist season had not begun and I had the roads and the villages almost as much to myself as in the good old days of the horse. That was indeed a wonderful fortnight for Cotswoldian objects and their settings—the gravity of all those stone buildings in buff and grey offset by radiant blossom in garden and orchard, the oaks in their gold-before-green overture (it was a year of "the oak before the ash") and the great horse chestnuts in full bridal array.

As I went from place to place I gained one firm impression that remained with me to the end, namely, that the Cotswold country was the last real bit of old England left. It has maintained a wholesome unself-conscious pride in its own well-being sufficient to preserve it naturally without the need of such artificial measures as "designation" or "preservation orders". The first thing that must strike anyone who moves about in the district is the way in which it has survived the timber-greed of two wars and subsequent peace-times with so many hardwood trees still standing in

9

woods, in parks, in long roadside avenues, in byeway hedgerows, and even in open fields. The economic coniferous plantations which now blotch countrysides, once so fair, including our National Parks, are almost entirely absent.

The next thing one notices is the number of old manor-houses (and nearly every village has one) which are still occupied by private persons and not, as elsewhere, either marked for demolition or in use by an institution or a department of local or national government. Then there are the road-sides, still edged with generous grass margins where wild flowers can flourish abundantly. The effect of this is to make the approaches to, and the links between, villages separate features in their own right, full of interest and most rewarding to the traveller who has resisted the temptation to move fast.

(i) THE COTSWOLD STORY

It is a most favoured region now, and so it has been even in days before history was written. The greater folk of the Stone Age and of Romano-British times have left plenty of visible evidence of that, so have the Saxons, the Normans, and the great merchant princes of the fourteenth and fifteenth centuries when English wool ruled the market in the Western World. And now a new squirearchy has grown up in which you may find merchant adventurers of another sort—captains and lieutenants of industry whose sources of wealth lie elsewhere. They can afford to employ gardeners, stone-masons, and thatchers, and keep their houses and lands up to the unwritten Cotswold law of amenity, as pleasant for the stranger to see as the occupier to live in.

It is not only luck which has favoured the region with so many suc-cessive periods of prosperity. The hills are but one group in a long chain beginning with the Purbeck Hills on the English Channel and ending with the Cleveland Hills on the Yorkshire coast, but geography has given the Cotswolds the best place in the whole range or at any rate one which happened to fit in with successive events in our history like a dovetail.

The western escarpment overlooks the lower Severn and its estuary which gave access to the great maritime adventures of the late Stone Age some two thousand years or more before the birth of Christ. They settled on either shore; but their tombs (long barrows) are more numerous on the Cotswold uplands than elsewhere.

The Romans consolidated the first stage of their conquest of Britain by halting at this natural barrier which so conveniently formed an oblique line across country from south-west to north-east and made all along it a frontier road, now called the Fosse Way, which goes from Ilchester to Lincoln, deviating only six miles out of the straight in the two hundred between these places. Along this it was in the Cotswolds that they made their principal strategic road-junction. Here, again, geography was no doubt the first thought. Farther penetration to the west could best be made at the lowest convenient crossing of the Severn, which was where an island lay in mid-stream at the site of the present town of Gloucester. This, then, was the objective of the great main road from London through Silchester. It crossed the Fosse Way at Corinium (now Cirencester), made straight for the ridge escarpment which it reached at Birdlip, nine hundred feet above the Severn Valley, and continued, regardless of gradient, down the famous Birdlip Hill to their new forward base.

The importance of the junction at Cirencester was augmented some-what later by a second road from London (Akeman Street) coming via St. Albans, and the place became an important centre of the local Celtic tribe (Dobuni), a market town and school (if one may use that word broadly) of Roman culture. As a result, their chiefs or rich magnates built those great courtyard establishments known as *villas*, more than twelve of which have been discovered within a short distance of the town, with bye-roads linking them to it. The best preserved is at Chedworth, owned by the National Trust, and many more are distributed throughout the Cots-wolds, whose configuration lent itself ideally to the siting of these houses (partly domestic, partly farming, partly industrial) which flourished ex-ceedingly until the decline of the Empire.

This second golden age, which must have begun to fade at the beginning of the fifth century, was destroyed by the English at a single blow when the Saxon chief, Ceawlin, won the decisive battle of Deoram (now Dyrham, near Bristol) in the year 577 and then sacked the three Roman towns of

11

Bath, Gloucester, and Cirencester. Thereafter, the Cotswolds were annexed by the important tribe of Hwicce which formed one of the early Saxon kingdoms and has left its name in the Forest of Wychwood.

As West Cotswold with its high ground had offered special attractions to the Neolithic folk who had sailed up the Bristol Channel, so the East, opposite in every way, had all that could be desired by the English intruder. Here the ground rises gently from the Vale of the White Horse, where ships from the German Ocean could then penetrate up the Thames at least as far as Cricklade. Tributaries of that river coming out of the Cotswolds would also have been navigable at that time for a considerable distance. These tributaries issue from valleys which must indeed have delighted the heart of the agriculturally-minded Saxon. They wind far up into the hills from sources near the western escarpment, along which lie the highest points of the range, so that where the uplands are most exposed the valleys are deepest and most sheltered. Moreover, the bottoms of these valleys are roomy and the streams have but a gentle fall giving nearly level sites for village settlement and plenty of water for mills and fish-traps.

So the English became possessed of the Hills in the seventh century and consolidated their gains, the successful tribe of the Hwicce spreading themselves as far as Worcester, though their small kingdom was presently merged in the large and powerful one of Mercia. But the hill folk preserved a strong separate individuality—as they still do—uncorrupted even by the formation of shires. At the present time the Cotswolds are divided between Worcestershire, Oxfordshire, Wiltshire, and Gloucestershire, the latter having the lion's share. There was still further parcelling in early days, when Winchcomb and Cirencester staked out their own little shires; but it is the regional rather than the county allegiance which makes itself both felt and seen wherever you go.

A long time elapsed between the heyday of the Roman villas and that of the great clothiers and woolstaplers, when the Cotswolds once more became news on the page of history though, judging by what remains of contemporary works carried out after the tenth century, in the parish churches, the level of prosperity was high and of a settled sort. In promoting and upholding this, geography again played an important rôle. The western

12

cliffs of Mid and North Cotswold overlook that very fertile country where the Avon flows from Stratford through the Vale of Evesham to join the Severn at Tewkesbury. It was, as it still is, a land as rich in fertility as any in the whole of England. But in those days its fortunes were so closely knit with those of the Cotswolds as to make it a sort of bank of "capital reserve", which must have helped considerably to promote and maintain the woollen industry which gave the Cotswolds a leading place in all Europe in the fourteenth and fifteenth centuries and made the fortunes of those merchant princes who returned thanks to God in stone and lie in effigy with folded hands on the pavements of the churches they rebuilt.

The nature of this tie was religious rather than commercial and came about through the number of large monasteries (and those among the most important in Britain) which had established themselves beside the lower reaches of the Avon and the Severn. Here stood the great Bene-dictine houses of Evesham, Pershore, Tewkesbury, and Gloucester. Another large house of the same order stood at Winchcombe within the outlying spurs of the hills, and the Cistercian Abbey of Hailes lay near it at the opening of one of the short valleys in the escarpment. These communities owned much property in the hills as well as on the low ground and the Cistercians, who specialized in sheep-farming, must have been largely responsible for improving the famous local breed.

## (ii) BUILDINGS

That chain of hills, of which Cotswold is a member, is all formed of a limestone of Jurassic age which yields some of the best building-stone in England. Its quarries supplied the fabric for most of our old cathedrals, notwithstanding the difficulties and hazards of primitive transport. The stone was even exported to Dublin in the thirteenth century to build the metropolitan Church of St. Patrick. It varies in degree of hardness (often in the same quarry) and in its durability in weathering, when built, and it varies in colour from a warm, tawny buff to a nearly pure white. The yellowish tone, commonly found in the native rock, usually turns grey on exposure to the air but is sometimes permanent.

13

The characteristic formation is the *roe-stone* (to use the old English word, that is, of an appearance resembling the roe of a fish, which is a more exact and graphic description than the foreign *oolite* (egg-stone) preferred by geologists. Everywhere along that chain, ordinary parish churches and ordinary houses and cottages are found made of one or other variety of this stone and roofed with slabs of it. But elsewhere than in the Cotswolds these buildings are mixed with those of brick and, in any case, the majority are roofed with Welsh or Cumberland slates. Only in this region is there almost complete uniformity, whole villages as well as solitary farmsteads (with their outbuildings) being made of the local stone—wall and roof.

On this visit I was immensely impressed by the conservation of ancient types of structure, of which the more obvious are the mullioned window and old English gable. Houses and cottages still follow fashions set in the sixteenth and seventeenth centuries, and so closely that it is quite hard to distinguish ancient from modern. So far as mullioned windows are concerned one may think that this is not entirely due to traditionalism, for the roe-stone with all its virtues has not great tensile strength. In windows of medieval design (round-headed or pointed) made with separate arch-stones the problem does not arise, nor does it with the mullioned window where there is only a small interval between vertical bars. But in the sash-window the opening is too great for the lintel to stand the strain and it will generally be seen that in houses of the eighteenth and nineteenth centuries which have adopted such windows the lintels are of wood. It is more remarkable that the mullioned windows should still retain their dripstones as in the Tudor days (then a direct heritage of the Gothic styles), but these, too, give added strength as well as ornament.

The gabling of all sorts of buildings is most remarkable and the additional skill and labour involved in carrying out such sub-roofs at right angles to the main ones seems to have caused local craftsmen no concern at all. One knows that in the ordinary blue-slate roof the greatest care has to be taken to ensure that such junctions, or "valleys", do not leak and a lead flashing is tucked in under the edges of the slates. The Cotswold slater did not use any such adjunct. His stone slabs were so laid that,

14

normally, joins made more than two centuries ago are still watertight. Another device not seen in blue slate roofs is the way in which the edges on approaching the eaves are swept into a slightly concave curve. This breaks the abruptness of the roof-to-wall angle and adds a delightful touch both to gable and frontage.

But the most characteristic individual building is the farmyard barn. This is obviously an ecclesiastical inheritance and many samples of the prototype monastic tythebarn still remain, including the largest one in England. What is so astonishing is that nearly every farm-house has one, that it is true to type even if only erected within fairly recent years, and that it is often larger than the parish church. Like the tythebarn, it has a porch built like a transept with folding doors which revolve on the ancient pin-and-socket principle. The opening is large enough to admit a fully loaded hay-wain. Frequently one sees a barn with a transeptal porch on either side, giving it the cruciform plan, and sometimes one or more aisles have been added. In all cases the gable-ends have been nicely finished with a coping of well-dressed stone with a short finial at the apex. But in the large porches of eighteenth- and nineteenth-century date a hipped roof usually takes the place of the gable.

Although good freestone is so readily available and the all-stone village is so characteristic it is rare to find any building except the church older than the sixteenth century, and most of the "old-looking" houses date from the seventeenth. I have not found any clue as to what the structures were made of that these houses replaced; most likely it was half-timber of which there are some scattered examples, a style doubtless shamed out of existence by local fashion-bias. The thatched roof is still to be seen—notably at Minster Lovell—and thatching is still a living craft, though its exponents are few and mainly located in the Vale of Evesham.

(iii) PARISH CHURCHES

These are a most interesting and representative collection in which well-developed specimens of all the Gothic styles are found, though there is little post-Reformation work. In general, especially on the eastern side, the churches established by the Anglo-Saxons seem to have escaped the passion for demolition and renovation under the first century of Norman rule, and most of the Norman work found is of late and transitional character. It is the latter which predominates, and those restorers were more content to leave bits of Saxon work intact than their predecessors had been.

Of Early English work there is a good deal and the transition between this and the Decorated style is well marked at Stow-on-the-Wold, where two perfect examples of text-book "plate tracery" can be seen in the north aisle, and the west window with its unusual reticulated design inset with trefoils is probably not much later. Specimens of the Decorated style are chiefly confined to the lesser churches, except at Witney, as the larger ones are mainly the result of rebuildings at the height of wool prosperity. Longborough has a south transept of the late fourteenth century with fine flowing tracery and Cheltenham an astonishing wheel window of that time. There are several sanctus bell-cotes.

There is a good deal of Perpendicular work both in the lesser and the larger churches, ranging from the late fourteenth to the early sixteenth centuries. Winchcomb and the nave at Cirencester have the most orthodox version of the style, Northleach and Chipping Campden are a later varient. Still later is Fairford and the unique three-storied porch-with-guildhall at Cirencester and latest of all (mid-sixteenth century) the great tower of St. Sampson's, Cricklade.

When it is borne in mind that the Perpendicular style had its origin in the great church of the Abbey of St. Peter at Gloucester (now the Cathedral), the Cotswold examples, so near the source, have added interest. The fan vault was also invented at Gloucester and two good specimens of this are to be seen at Cirencester; another, complete with contemporary windows with some of their original glass, is in a chantry chapel at North Leigh. This church, on the eastern fringe of the hills, is representative of all the stages of architectural evolution, beginning with its Saxon tower and ending with its eighteenth-century Perrot Chapel.

A local feature, repeated in many churches, is the inclusion of a stone shelf in the piscina-niche. Another is a niche on the east wall of the porch. At Aldworth this niche has holes sunk in the sill, evidently for the support of wax lights.

# II  EVENLODE AND WINDRUSH

I BEGAN my refresher-course by going to stay with friends over Eastertide who lived on rising ground in the lower Valley of the Evenlode and within a mile of the large partly excavated Roman villa of North Leigh. When my friend first came to live in these parts he was thrilled to find one morning in his garden one of those very large snails with the pale porcelain-like shell which has earned the name of Roman snail because, in its limited and local range in this country, it is generally closely associated with Roman remains. This variety (*Helix Pomatia*) is still regarded as a table delicacy in France and Italy, so the conclusion that it was imported from the Continent by our Latin conquerors to remain for us a living link with Romano-British culture seems an obvious one, though I believe modern zoologists have attempted to debunk it. The creature certainly looks much more imperial than our common garden snail and is an interesting member of the Cotswold fauna.

Just across the river from the Roman villa are the huge quarries of Stonesfield whose product was the limestone roofing slate of the best quality prepared by the lengthy operation of "frosting", that is, hoarding the slabs taken from the quarry (or rather the mine, for the workings were underground) in earthen clamps to preserve the "sap" until the winter. At the coming of the first frost they were exhumed, spread out over the ground, and left for the freezing to start natural cleavages which the slatter would complete artificially as soon as milder weather set in. If the all-important first frost should give no sign of its approach until after dark, but then be detected, the ringers would be summoned to the church belfry to rouse the village and every able-bodied man and boy would turn out of their beds to spread the slabs. Mr. W. J. Arkell* believes that this process was not discovered until the end of the sixteenth century. It produced a much thinner and lighter slate than the natural flag-stone used before that time and got from many local quarries. The beds at Stonesfield were particularly amenable to this treatment and (next to Colley Weston in Northamptonshire) the place became the principal centre for stone roofing material. An early example of the Stonesfield frosted slate and its lasting

*Oxford Stone                    17

properties is seen in the roofs of Wadham College, Oxford, made in 1612.

The quarries have now been closed for more than half a century except to fossil-hunters, for whom treasures rarer than gold may lurk. It is in these beds that remains of the earliest known mammal was discovered, a rat-like animal, but surely the most venerable of all our ancestors. Only one or two specimens have been recovered—bits of jaw-bone, all found here. They keep company with the remains of the dodo in that unique architectural curiosity, the University Museum at Oxford. Every Cotswold village is roofed with Cotswold stone of one sort or another, but at Stonesfield itself alien materials in red and purple are conspicuous. This irony arises because architects in need of Stonesfield slates for restorations or even new work, failing to get what they wanted from the quarries, have bought the complete roofs of houses in the village.

A little higher up the Evenlode Valley is the last remaining thicket of the ancient forest of Wychwood, whose name (as already mentioned) conserves the memory of those early Saxon conquerors, the Tribe Hwicce. Until 1862 Wychwood was as large and important a royal chase as the New Forest and stretched out westward over all the high ground between the Evenlode and Windrush valleys, overhanging the villages of Ascot, Shipton, and Milton—all of them still named on the map "under Wychwood". But then Queen Victoria decided to part with it in the interests of agricultural improvement, probably at the instigation of her late husband who had been bent on a forward policy in land development. And so, in the year named, it was disafforested and sold in lots. A portion adjoining Cornbury Park was bought by the owners of that estate and thus saved. The rest was grubbed up and the village of Leafield, once in a clearing near the middle of the forest, is now on the open downs and its church (one of Gilbert Scott's most elaborate but least successful works) is a landmark that can be seen for miles. The village cross strikes a more devotional note. In 1873 a new shaft was placed in its ancient base "by the inhabitants of Leafield as a memorial of their delivery from the scourge of smallpox".

It was a great thing to have saved even that much of Wychwood and to have allowed that relic (a heritage of the primeval forest of Britain) to remain so wild. My hostess drove me past its northern limit which lies on the Charlbury-Burford road. Just below there, in the Evenlode Valley, is the little church of Shorthampton which stands detached in a narrow lane without any visible sign of a parish to support it. Though very small, it has managed to amass a fair sample of every architectural style from Norman to Perpendicular and some years ago, on removal of its whitewash skin, the medieval paintings were recovered in nearly every part of nave and chancel. They were in a fairly fresh state but are now beginning to grow indistinct. The artistry is crude but the subject matter unusual. One picture represents the story found in the Apocrypha in which the child Christ models clay sparrows and then breathes life into them so that they fly away. We went on to Idbury church to see a brass on which the emblems of the mason's craft appear and then down over the watershed into the Windrush Valley to Taynton, where my hostess dropped me to spend the rest of the day.

The day in question was Easter Bank Holiday, so I had rejected the kind offer of my hostess to provide me with a picnic lunch believing that this was an occasion when food would be available everywhere, especially in a district much favoured by motorists like the Cotswolds. I had never been to Taynton before but it was an objective I had long wished to reach, for along the valley of the Coombe Brook, which flows into the village, are situated a long range of quarries which have supplied the famous Taynton stone for at least as far back as 1086, when they were first put on record in Domesday Book. Innumerable houses, churches, and bridges in the near neighbourhood have come from there. In the fourteenth century, over two thousand tons went down the Thames from Lechlade to Windsor for improvements to the Castle that William of Wykeham was making there, who also used the stone in his New College, as did the builders of several other Oxford colleges. Blenheim Palace also came out of the Coombe Valley.

But Taynton village was, in itself, a most attractive place. There was nothing about it to suggest the twentieth century or even Easter Bank

19

Holiday. It seemed to have grown up on the valley bottom on a completely irregular plan, unfathomable to the stranger. Its walls, houses, and outhouses, all in silver-grey, appeared at different levels through gaps in spring foliage and blossom, and not a motor-car or another visitor besides myself was stirring anywhere. That visitors were not even expected was plain from the fact that there was nowhere to get anything to eat. Nobody "catered for the tourist", though I was told that the Rectory had just been sold and its new lay owners intended to do so. However, the mistress of the post-office shop (though officially closed) kindly provided me with two small apple tartlets in cardboard boxes out of her stock. Such frugality was more than counterbalanced by the discovery of an English place which could still be so self-sufficient as to give no thought to the holidaymaker.

At the end of the village is a large handsome farm-house where the Lee family live who own the lower half of the valley in which about half of the ancient quarries are situated, though overgrown and masked in one place by a large wood. Just beyond that is the one most recently opened. It is worked by Mr. Philip Lee and an assistant and they are the sole survivors of the great army of men who raised Taynton stone in the Coombe Valley since before the Norman Conquest. Being the day it was, I found Mr. Lee at work there all alone but kindly disposed to spare some time to show me round and talk. He said that he had worked at the stone here on the family land since he was a boy (when he first resolved to keep the quarrying going), learning the art "the hard way" by trial and error and picking up what he could from old men who had spent their lives there in the busier days. But for years he had only had one assistant and, between them, they had carried out the large and important contract for the new Bodleian Library at Oxford, where the stone is used to line the walls of vestibule and corridors and to form a dado on the staircase. W. J. Arkell says of this work: "The grain of the stone is most beautiful, and the carved frieze on both storeys is proof of its tractability. This local stone has proved itself in interior work not only more fitting but more beautiful than the costly travatines and marbles so often used—for instance inside the new London University building at Bloomsbury."*

*Oxford Stone

Of course, if Mr. Lee had not been true to the idealist aim he formed in boyhood they would never have got this famous Taynton stone for the new Bodleian. But his name does not appear in the list of artists, craftsmen, and contractors printed in the official book issued at the time of the opening ceremony. No doubt it was a great honour for him to have the result of his own labour and a slice of his own land made part and parcel of a monument of European distinction, but he was not one of the many who made any financial gain out of it. I gathered that the reverse was the case.

Late in the afternoon I walked the two miles into Burford where Easter Monday was being properly observed and motor coaches from distant parts were still putting down as well as picking up. It had begun to rain and groups of the disembarked, still preserving something of their coach-bound formations wandered up and down the wide High Street looking for something to look at.

This was quite a different Burford from what I remembered finding a few years before, which then struck me as one of the most dignified and enchanting places I had ever seen. Now it looked exceedingly grim and quite disillusioned about the beautifulness of growing old. And Burford is genuinely old. Like Chipping Campden, it has a number of domestic buildings which go back before the all-stone-house fashion days of the sixteenth and seventeenth centuries. But Campden has the sort of lay-out like the Royal Mile at Edinburgh which is perfect for purposes of secular pilgrimage—you see everything worth seeing as you go your way and at the end find the *chef d'oeuvre*, which is the great parish church. At Burford, the new way into the town from Oxford and London (along the high ground above the town) is not the same as the old one, which followed the Windrush, and the *chef d'oeuvre*, which is (again) the parish church, has to be looked for. In fact, for Burford, you need plenty of time, a little sunshine, and no coach-parties.

For any river "Windrush" would be a delightful name and, for the stream which owns it, it is a particularly happy and suggestive one and shows what can be done by leaving a name alone for a few centuries to be tongue-moulded without playing any academic tricks with it. The word was evidently coined by the Ancient Briton in pre-Roman days and meant neither wind nor rushes; but in its Anglicized form it adds a touch of magic both to itself and its environment. Anyone must feel this who visits those singularly romantic little villages which lie near it on its winding course between Burford and Witney—Fulbrook, Swinbrook, Asthall, and Minster Lovell.

Swinbrook church contains a unique pair of funereal monuments in which six members of the Fettiplace family, once lords of the manor, recline in tiers on vault-like shelves. Each monument contains three effigies, but one is Jacobean and the other late seventeenth century. The former represents ancestors who expired in the reigns of Henry VII, Elizabeth, and James, but all have like hair-styles and are rigidly accoutred in similar suits of armour of the last period. A Gothic angel holding a shield of arms (outmoded almost a century) forms the key-stone of the arch above. The figures in the other monument make allowance for change of fashion, the uppermost one wearing a wig with his armour and having an antique helmet placed at his disposal. All are carved in a local free-stone and the monuments have the unusual advantage over most of their kind in being endowed with a fund to keep them in good preservation. It brings in about ten pounds a year which enables them to be dusted and cleaned and the tinctures and gilding on their heraldry to be freshened from time to time. And there is much else of interest in this little church, besides.

At Witney one link with the old Cotswold wool trade survives unbroken and in full vigour. Here, the making of blankets has been a speciality from times out of mind, and it used to be said that the high quality of the local product was due to the nature of Windrush water. But this may be just another magical property of the river likely to escape the scientific analyst.

The visitor to Witney should not think he has seen all until he has been to Cogges. There is a way to it by road, but it is far better to walk. The way lies through a narrow alley close to the old market-house and butter-cross. Then, in less than a hundred yards, you are right out of the town and in open water-meadows, through which the Windrush, divided into two

22

branches, flows. Substantial bridges carry the footpath over, which leads to a group of buildings lying at the dead end of a lane coming down from the Witney-Eynsham road. They consist of a manor-house, a little church with an octagonal tower and pointed cap, and a parsonage house closely adjoining it, partly of thirteenth-century date.

The church was presented to the Abbey of Fécamp in Normandy in the twelfth century and a cell was established there, a prior and one or two monks residing. When Henry IV dissolved the alien priories the monks were sent home and it was taken into the King's hands, his grandson, Henry VI, presenting it to his new foundation of Eton College. The thing of special interest is the large chantry chapel on the north side, a work of the fourteenth century, which shows clear signs of having been carried out by French masons with some regard for English architectural conventions. It has a frieze carved with large and boldly executed figures representing animals fighting with human weapons and defending themselves with small target-like shields. Now, at Swinbrook, there is a set of stalls in the chancel (which one would not expect to find in a small parish church with no collegiate or monastic associations) and on one of their misericords is a man holding out just such a shield as one sees here. Another has a man holding what looks like an ox-goad, but pointed at either end. I confess that the allusion in each case is lost on me. I have never seen anything like these weapons in English church carvings except at Cogges. Did the stalls come from there? And is the story behind these battling creatures a French and not an English legend?

Incidentally, the manor of Cheltenham also belonged to Fécamp. The Abbey was forced to accept it in exchange for Rye by Edward I who wished to get rid of all French satellites on the coast of the English Channel.

# III VALLEYS OF THE EASTERN SLOPE

I NOW went by train from Witney to Fairford *en route* for Cricklade, towards which place my bicycle had been shaping a leisurely course "per goods". I have not discovered why they took the trouble to build a line from Oxford to Fairford, seeing how shy the railways were of serving the Cotswolds. They did not even venture a line up the Windrush Valley, which would certainly have developed Burford to their mutual interest and have gone on without much difficulty to Winchcomb, providing a proper East-West link to Cheltenham and Gloucester. Fairford is chiefly noted for its church and its trout-fishing. Even so, the railway stopped short of reaching the town by more than a mile. Between Fairford and Cricklade there is neither rail nor bus connection and, if my future hostess of the White Hart had not offered to rescue me in her own car, I should have had to taxi those six miles or try to match trains from Witney to Oxford, Oxford to Swindon, Swindon to Cricklade. This, however, was only a mild foretaste of the extraordinary difficulty of getting about in the Cotswolds by means of public transport.

The church of St. Mary at Fairford has as much to interest the ordinary sightseer as the ecclesiologist. With its stained glass and fittings it survived the Reformation in a more complete state than any other of our parish churches. The only important feature conspicuously missing is the rood-loft, though how it was arranged is plain to see, the three shallow recesses high up above the western tower-arch show exactly where the figures of the rood were placed. The contemporary glass in the twenty-eight windows is almost complete and it is fairly certain that it came from the same workshops at Westminster which supplied that for King's College Chapel, Cambridge. The woodwork is also in a good state of preservation, roofs, parclose screens (with slight restorations), and stalls with misericords. These number fourteen (one of them frankly in the Rabelaisian class). The fine tomb of John Tame, the rich woolstapler of Cirencester, who rebuilt the church in its present form and died in the year 1500 before it was quite finished, is intact with its brass and inscriptions. Strong sunshine brings out not only the colour of the glass but also the now faint tinctures of saints and angels and other decoration with which the walls were covered.

In rebuilding the church, the lower part of what was originally a Norman tower was left standing and given a new upper stage (the part of it seen from outside). It is a bold and original conception in tower-design; and it is rather remarkable that the architect has resisted anything like slavish copying of the other large Cotswold churches, rebuilt so short a time before and whose virtues must have been on every man's lips, especially those of patron woolstaplers.

Few parish churches enjoy a more perfect setting. Standing on a rise in a large clear green space, it has a park of tall well-grown trees to the north, to the west a placid reach of the River Coln, to the east it looks across the broad High Street towards a range of old stone houses, built only on the far side. Just below, to the south, is the wide market square where the inns signed "George" and "Bull" stand. The latter is famous among anglers for the stretch of trout water it preserves on the Coln, where it also owns an island cultivated as a pleasance and a kitchen-garden, the latter guarded by a stuffed fox with glaring eyes.

Cricklade, like Fairford, is rather on the fringe of the Cotswolds than "in" them, though both have the characteristic stone buildings with some in half-timber. Judged by its size and its shops, Cricklade seems much more of a village than a town, yet it has two parish churches, both ancient, one of them on the magnificent scale comparable with Fairford and Cirencester. The place is situated on the Roman Ermine Street and was formerly the highest point that was navigable on the Thames, which now runs as a mere brook below the town, a decline not due to natural causes but the making of a canal in the late eighteenth century to connect the Thames with the Severn. This started from Lechlade and diverted first the water and then the trade. The Thames and Severn Canal was opened in 1793. It is now derelict, but the feeders have not been returned to their old courses above Cricklade, and Lechlade remains the highest point, even for boating.

The smaller church of St. Mary has some interesting Norman work and would, I expect, attract more visitors if it were not for the much larger St. Sampson's which stands on the hill-top at the head of the town, distracting the eyes of the newcomer. All periods are represented in this great cruciform church, from Transitional Norman to Perpendicular work so late as to be outside the limit usually set for the last phase of Gothic building. This is found in the tower, as rebuilt in the middle of the sixteenth century, and the circumstance of its construction is closely bound up with a poignant historical event.

The builder of the tower was that ambitious and utterly unscrupulous John Dudley, Duke of Northumberland, who had been made Protector in the latter part of the reign of King Edward VI. He allied himself to the royal house by marrying his son, Lord Guildford Dudley, to the Lady Jane Grey, great grand-daughter of Henry VII and, furthermore, persuaded the young king to name this lady in his will as his successor, to the exclusion of his sisters, Mary and Elizabeth; the plea being that only in this way could the continuance and safety of the Protestant faith be made secure in England in the event of Edward's death. Everyone knows how the plot failed and brought the conspirator, together with the Nine Days' Queen and many innocent victims, to the block.

Shortly before these events, Dudley had bought the manor of Cricklade (which must, at that time have had some valuable connection with the Cotswold wool trade). Whether he found the tower of the great church in ruin or dismantled it in order to raise the present one does not appear. But the result is much more like a personal monument than anything raised to the glory of God. The interior, right up to the high stone vault, is encrusted with the heraldic badges and emblems of the builder. The whole is on a very grand scale with octagonal turret-buttresses and elaborate exterior panelling, and it poses two riddles. Why did Dudley build such a costly thing in a newly acquired manor so far from his family estates? Any why, if he was (at court) such a powerful champion of Protestantism, did he sanction the use of certain ornaments associated with the old faith and have a rood-loft stair built in? Did he call his tower to witness when he tried to beg his life from Mary, protesting that he had always been Catholic at heart?

But the oldest thing about the church is its dedication, for Sampson was a saint of the early Celtic Church. He has only two other dedications in England—both in Cornwall—and is best remembered at Dol in Brittany. It signifies that Christian worship was practised on that site so long ago as the sixth century, even before the invasion of the Cotswolds by the Saxons.

My bicycle had duly reached the "White Hart" before I got there and my plan was to work my way up along the eastern side of the Hills towards the northern extremity in leisurely rides, and then down the other side, returning to base by some form of public transport each night. This worked all right the first few days. Later, I found it took the whole morning, and by most circuitous routes (no matter how early the start) to rejoin my mount.

I had heard that the last flock of pure-bred Cotswold sheep was owned by a farmer at Aldsworth—Mr. Garne. I hoped to see this historic animal to which England once owed so much and set my first course in that direction. The great thing about travelling on a bicycle, rather than in a motor-car, is that in the latter one always appears to be tied to time. Motoring creates the illusion that *time* is more important than *place*—much more! Consequently, there is never any time either to stop or to stray. On a bicycle one is completely liberated from this inhibition, and so I had hardly gone more than a mile along the great Roman trunk road of Ermine Street before I strayed. This was to investigate a solid looking church which stood by itself, except for a large parsonage, about half a mile off on the right-hand side. It serves the parish of Latton-cum-Eisey and has some fine Transitional Norman work with interesting detail and corbel heads of late Gothic as roof brackets worth a glance, yet I don't suppose it is on the visiting list of many tourists and passers by on that great fast road. Even if spying it, they would fear to lose time by stopping.

The next turning takes one to Down Ampney from whence another bye-road goes due north for several miles to the Coln Valley near Bibury. Here, although the ground was doing little more than beginning to swell into a gentle roll, I felt myself to be "in" the Cotswolds. I passed some new council houses which were evidently planned on that assumption— and there was also the name of the place. There is a distinct tendency in

27

the Cotswolds to group places in one valley under the name of its river and to put that name first. It is a local idiosyncrasy and perhaps goes back to the days of the first Anglo-Saxon settlement when families worked their way up the courses of streams (already named by their Celtic predecessors) and the river name naturally took precedence of the other. Thus, there are a string of Colns and Duntisbornes and, here, a string of Ampneys along the Ampney Brook above Down Ampney—Ampney St. Peter, Ampney St. Mary, Ampney Crucis. As to the council houses (and the new buildings in general), I found at least one rule had been universally observed in the Cotswolds, namely, that in appearance they should be as little disturbing as possible to the established order of all-stone buildings. In a very few instances the traditional materials have been used, Cotswold stone in house and garden walls and Cotswold slate on the roof; but chiefly one sees artificial stone in walls and concrete slates on the roof. These have been toned to a light buff, like stone fresh from the quarry, and the manufacturer has somehow been able to produce an effect which seems to me much better than is seen where synthetic materials are used elsewhere. Some of the great barns re-slated in this way look very well. In what I suppose to be cheaper construction, a buff-toned brick is used. This, too, unlike the old-fashioned yellow brick, succeeds tolerably well in being inoffensive. So that, visually speaking, a degree of harmony is maintained between the old and the new throughout the region that, while exceedingly pleasant to the stranger, must surely have its effect on the social life of resident communities.

At Poulton I felt myself to be properly in the Cotswolds. It is not a show place but it has some nice studies in gabling and roofing. Northward again I passed through two named cross-roads, Betty's Grave and Ready Token, the former recalling some sad tale of suicide, the latter a vanished licence. Ready Token is a five-cross roads on Akeman Street, the more northerly Roman route from Cirencester to London via St. Albans. One of the side-roads coming in from the direction of Fairford and seeming to aim west is called Welsh Way and may, like Buckle Street farther north, have been in use before the coming of the Romans and given its present name (probably recalling the Welsh cattle drovers) much later. The

28

antiquary who is interested in discovering the origin of country roads would find a rich field for research here where prehistoric, Roman and medieval systems of communication were all well developed.

I approached Bibury with mixed feelings. I had never been there but often heard it named as one of "our beauty-spots", a magnetic description whose attractive power has usually destroyed original virtue. I don't know what it may look like in a more advanced state of the season but on that particular day of little traffic and bright spring sunshine I found it good and full of pleasant surprises. It is a double village with Bibury (which owns the parish church and has monopolized the postal address) on the left bank of the River Coln and Arlington on the right. The two are laid out quite differently, Arlington occupying a hillside and Bibury a long river frontage with a market square at one end, adjoining the church and the manor-house. The valley is flat-bottomed and the broad water-meadow lying between the two places (made an island by the river and the mill-stream), has no building on it at the upper end, though at the lower, where there is a long causeway, there stands a row of old houses with Cotswold gables in peaks and sweeps like the illustration to a fairy tale. This is Arlington Row, built for cloth-workers in the seventeenth century and now owned by the National Trust, but still tenanted.

Behind Arlington Row the right bank turns sharply, closing the valley gap and making a background to the view. It becomes steep as a cliff and is wooded with tall trees. Towards it, the river, spanned by a three-arch bridge, runs by the road and houses on the left bank in a long placid stretch, reflecting the woods and stone buildings in a manner that makes the setting seem peculiarly rich and solemn like an oil-painting of a century ago. A subject calling for swans; and, in fact, they are there!

Nor is the church disappointing. It has an unusually tall chancel-arch with carved Saxon imposts, a rare thing that I could only compare with that of St. Mary-in-Castro in Dover Castle. Other pre-Conquest work is there, too. Transitional Norman, which, I have already said, is to be seen in nearly all the East Cotswold churches, is represented here by a particularly beautiful feature. This is the north doorway. It is in two orders, the outer round-headed with typical twelfth-century chevron and billet

29

ornament; the inner, forecasting the coming change to Early English, with a trefoil head.

Above the village is a trout hatchery. Past this I took my way up stream towards Coln Rogers through the hamlet of Ablington which, though very small, has two notable houses, one, I was told, had been built by a wool magnate in the last year of King Henry VII. A successor had re-made the front in Jacobean style. House and gardens were kept up in the best Cotswold manner which would surely have delighted the occupiers of four centuries ago, as would the still unspoilt view over the wooded Coln Valley from those windows. The other is an Elizabethan manor-house with a barn-yard full of outbuildings no less quaint and spacious than itself.

My plan of the morning, to see the last flock of pedigree Cotswold sheep had not worked out. When within three miles of Aldsworth, I went into a telephone kiosk, looked up Mr. Garne's number, and introduced myself to his wife who answered the call. He was away that day, but I would be welcome to come another time. So I had to discover how far I could take my bicycle and get back to base by other means. The only bus service from any of the Coln villages was run by a Bibury man and this only on market-day to Cirencester. Two trains a day stopped at Chedworth and to catch the second of these, "the evening train", was my only chance.

The church at Coln Rogers is one of those which has the rare distinction of being the same shape as it was before the Battle of Hastings for, at all corners of nave and chancel, the stones are set in the manner called long-and-short that has never been used since Saxon times. Here, too, was the typical pilaster-strip with a typical Saxon sundial carved on it. There are many other things to see, including a pre-Reformation pulpit in local stone. But the importance of time was now beginning to preponderate over place and I had to hurry off up stream again to Coln St. Denis.

There is a besetting snare in going from one to another of these Cotswold villages. The cottages with their gables, well-made chimneys, mullioned windows, and trim gardens, and the great barns with their enormous porches and stone roofs, properly finished off with coping-stones and finials, are all so admirable when seen for the first time. But constant repetition tends to blind one to their virtues. Yet, though there is close kinship in the local types, there is no such thing as "sameness". The buildings are individuals, and their arrangement and setting full of variety. If one can just avoid that snare of getting used to good appearances and taking them for granted, these differences can be enormously enjoyed *at sight* but are very difficult to describe.

Coln Rogers and Coln St. Denis are both "charming" villages, but their "charm" is more lightsome than Bibury, which could be called "picturesque", as I have tried to show, in the literal sense. These three and all other settlements in the Coln Valley, from Chedworth to Fairford, have something indefinable in common, which they would not have, had they evolved elsewhere—the *genius* of the Coln River, the Romans would have called it. I did reach Chedworth station just as the train was due, but no staff was present and the buildings locked up. The guard sold me a ticket and I left my bicycle on the platform and went off, first to Cirencester, then to Cricklade.

Next morning I was back again and found my old friend just where I had left him. Chedworth is chiefly known for its Roman villa, but though the villa is in the parish it is in quite a different place from the village. There is not even a direct road connecting them. By car you must make a detour of five miles. On foot you may take a very rough path with two or three stiles across it and be there within a mile and a half. But Chedworth village is quite worth visiting for its own sake. It is built all along a hillside which descends steeply into a wooded dingle. The long village street is high up. Below it are scattered houses with orchards. The church is at the very end, where the steep little valley, sending a tributary to the Coln, closes in against the green bosom of Chedworth Beacon. It looks as if the founder—whoever he was—had chosen this site as being near a spring of water for baptisms (a Celtic rather than a Saxon predilection) and that the village had grown from that point down valley towards the Fosse Way.

I remembered noticing when I was here before that there was a fifteenth-century date carved in Arabic numerals which used the half-eight symbol for the figure four, cut in a moulding of the south door. The convention is rather rare and of local occurrence.

# 1861, 1885, 1891.

This time I found two more, all on the south side—they are all the more interesting as being an exact record of the years when the south aisle was rebuilt and given its very large and fine windows in the last days of Perpendicular Gothic. The artist who worked the scalloped capitals of the Norman arcade had unusual ideas on variety. He managed to give this simple and universal pattern on the supports of only two arches twelve different treatments of detail.

To get on to Chedworth Roman villa I chose the rough footpath. It is indeed a rough one, and the stiles don't make a bicycle a good companion. But even with such handicaps this approach to the villa is well worth the trouble. It lies for half a mile through the thicket of Chedworth Wood, a contemporary environment which has remained constant and one which quietens and detaches the mind before arriving at the clearing where the ruins of the villa lie. Partly because of this natural background and partly because the works of preservation carried out by the National Trust are of a simple and unostentatious nature, the Chedworth villa stirs the imagination to an unusual degree. It is easy to raise the dead, to hear cross-talk in Latin and Welsh, and to feel how barbarous the English language would sound in their ears.

A little below the hollow where the villa lies, the River Coln runs. In this part of its course it is cutting through ground which rises more than 400 feet above its bed, and its valley is deep and imposing. On my way from there to Northleach I strayed a mile or two to the north to see the little church of Yanworth which stands on one side of a farmyard, with the farm-house opposite and a very fine barn of the best Cotswold type forming a third side.

Northleach was the chief meeting-place in all Cotswold for merchants and exporters of wool in the fifteenth century.* Its near rival was Chipping Campden. At both places the naves of their large churches were rebuilt at about the same time and in nearly the same style. I believe the same

* *The Wool Trade in English Mediaeval History*. Eileen Power.

32

masons' marks are found in the columns of each. While towers, porches, and window-tracery differ, the arcades are identical and the design is one which occurs only rarely, and nowhere else in a full-scale nave. The arcades have octagonal columns which carry the flattish four-centred arch which was common in the mid-fifteenth century. But the eight sides of the columns are given a hollow chamfer which is echoed in the moulded capitals above. When you look up at the latter they appear like eight-pointed stars which gives an exotic, almost oriental, touch to the whole interior, an effect, I confess, I have never liked. Both these churches, also those at Winchcomb and Cirencester, have a large traceried window filling what was formerly a blank space between the chancel arch and the clere-story roof. This formed the background for the rood figures and had usually been painted with a "Doom picture". To replace the solid wall with a screen of stained glass was doubtless an improvement. Where Northleach and Campden differ is in their towers and porches. Campden has a poor south porch, Northleach one of the finest in the whole country. Northleach has a well-designed tower in the normal idiom of the Per-pendicular style. That at Campden has a curious eccentricity (which I notice some people admire, but I think ugly). This is the joining of pairs of buttresses by an ogee arch just below the parapet, the apex carrying a pinnacle.

The Roman Fosse Way goes in a straight line from Cirencester to Northleach. It is a section of the long road that is well maintained and is crowded with both light and heavy traffic. The distance between the two places is 10 miles and there surely *must* be a bus connecting the two! But there isn't, and, of course, no railway station for miles. Having dumped my bicycle on a kindly inn-keeper I had to get a bus to Cheltenham (13¾ m.), then to Cirencester (15½ m.) and get on to Cricklade from there. I had found it impossible to learn the running times of any Bus Company except one. It published an easily accessible timetable but only operated a comparatively few routes. I hoped for better communications from Cirencester and moved my baggage there, to the Fleece Hotel, the next day. That very distinguished draughtsman, Sydney Jones, bestowed an eulogy on the "White Hart" at Cricklade in his *Thames Triumphant* which

I found it still deserved, though "real Wiltshire pig" is not so easy to serve for breakfast as it used to be.

After collecting my bicycle the next day at Northleach and ringing up Mr. Garne on the telephone I made my way to Aldsworth along the high ground above the Valley of the Leach where, in spite of its exposure to winter winds, there stand some very fine woods of beech. The Leach is not one of the exciting streams but it has the Cotswold way of giving its name to places—Northleach, Eastleach-Martin, Eastleach-Turville, Leach-lade.

Mr. Garne received me very kindly. He well remembered H. J. Massingham who took such an interest in his flock and wrote so enthusiastically about it. He was a fine type of man, a courteous but commanding figure; one could imagine the likes of him farming and trading wool in the olden time, when innumerable flocks of native strain grazed the Cotswold Hills. We went off to an immense field which had been sown with kale and swede turnips, the former with its succulent green branches standing a good eight feet high. Mr. Garne said that he had owned the last pedigree flock of Cotswold sheep, but now expenses of labour and "One thing and another" were so high that he had had to break it up and only retained a remnant. This came into view, penned among the kale and turnips, which they ate off the ground as they grew. The sight had to be seen to be believed, for the animals were enormous and their faces as well as their bodies were covered with long locks of wool through which their large melting eyes peeped. They reminded me of the eighteenth-century signwriter's idea of a "White Lion", hung over so many inns of that name. Mr. Garne's shepherd managed to catch and hold one of these powerful creatures while I cut off a lock from her shoulder as a souvenir. To the touch it was more like silk than wool. It has a regular ripple like a hairdresser's permanent wave and (without pulling the crinkles out) the length of staple measures eleven inches. The clip from one sheep weighs 14 to 17 pounds, and this wool still goes to make the best English worsted.

Aldsworth church has some interesting points. That local feature, the eastern niche in its large north porch, has holes sunk in the sill for wax lights. This porch is stone-vaulted and has its original outer door, which

34

is cut to form a small wicket—a thing seen in college gateways in the older universities, but rare in churches. In spite of this imposing entrance the church is quite small, but its medieval patron must have had a touch of megalomania for, when rebuilding that north aisle late in the fifteenth century, he caused gurgoyles and other ornament to be made on the Northleach scale.

My bicycle and I were now going to complete the day in each other's company all the way to Cirencester. Taking a rapid look at Coln St. Aldwyn and Quenington, and with the wind behind us for the first time, we went along in top gear down Roman Akeman Street, which has generous grass margins where cowslips grew in bunch-like clusters, and I don't remember seeing a single vehicle until we were nearly at the end of the journey.

# IV  NORTH COTSWOLD AND THE ESCARPMENT

THERE are few more impressive stretches of Roman road than the one which sets out north-west from Cirencester for Gloucester, reaching that city, founded at the chosen crossing of the Severn into South Wales with no appreciable variation in alignment (except the zig-zag on Birdlip Hill). The great modern road follows the line exactly (with a further easement at Birdlip) and one would think that in this passion for directness ease of gradient must suffer, but none of the switchbacks which bring you up the five-hundred-odd feet between Cirencester and Birdlip are really arduous.

The traveller who goes along this purposeful and uncompromising road, looking out over wolds which stretch to right and left, might never guess what charms of quite opposite character lie close to on either hand.

To the south of it is the valley of a little brook called the Duntisborne (*Dunsbourne*, I was told to call it by the Head Waitress of the "Fleece" who knew the traditional pronunciation, which is admittedly much bette for having its middle corner knocked off by generations of users). A very countrified road follows it in a pleasant rambling way which gives every chance to the small scenery for showing off its graces—and they are many. The string of settlements is quite different from those in the Coln Valley but hardly less attractive. You leave the Roman autobahn at Stratton and then proceed to find Daglingworth, Duntisborne Rous, Middle Duntisborne, Duntisborne Leer, and Abbot's Duntisborne.

Stratton church has a very crudely carved tympanum over the south door which is probably eleventh century. Antiquaries have suggested that it represents Daniel in the lions' den, but I think there is room for a better guess. At Daglingworth there is a fine barn which is a fair sample of the eighteenth-nineteenth century type, derived from the medieval model, seen in so many places. The porch gable is hipped, the huge doors have pin-and-socket hinges. There is a south aisle under a lean-to roof and the main roof is supported by four principals which have curved wall-posts springing from rough stone brackets. The church is of exceptional interest. Like Coln Rogers, all four corners of nave and chancel have Saxon long-and-short work, but in at least two corners they must have been rebuilt into new fabric at the restoration of 1845. Up to that date there had existed a short central tower containing a room with an altar—an exceedingly un-usual feature. This the restorers abolished though they preserved the altar which stands in a recess on the north side of the chancel. There is also a sundial, chancel-arch, three remarkable carvings, and a three-light window cut out of part of a Roman altar—all of Saxon date. A pretty feature is the eleventh-century doorway filled by an original fourteenth-century door with carved tracery.

The church at Duntisborne Rous is hardly less remarkable. It is a tiny building made picturesque by the addition of a small saddleback tower which contains its two original medieval bells, one calling for the prayers of the Virgin, the other of St. Catharine. Only a path leads to it, and the first builder seems to have chosen an unnecessarily awkward site, right over the brow of the hill where the ground is falling steeply towards the brook. You can see at a glance that in order to gain a level floor he

36

has had to build an undercroft below the chancel. In large churches such as those at Thirsk and Winchelsea this has been done because, presumably, the builders had to make the best of confined situations, and the lower rooms they turned to useful account as bone-houses. Here, the undercroft is not a structural necessity but a necessary structure. It is a genuine crypt chapel with all the proper parts—a stairway leading down from the chancel, a piscina, an aumbry, and a tiny Norman east window with moulded reveal.

The chancel is Norman as well as the crypt, but there are clear indications of an earlier regime, for there is long-and-short work to be seen and a large piece of herring-bone masonry in the north wall; the doorway has a triangular head. But that crypt seems to say that it marks a sacred site, possibly pre-Saxon, where a Celtic shrine had stood, another Cotswold relic of the ancient British Church—one calls to mind St. Sampson's at Cricklade and the parish church of Moreton-in-the-Marsh which still preserves a dedication to St. David.

The Duntisborne begins its course suddenly, opening the first cleft of its valley in the wold to nearly full depth all at once. On the high ground above its source, and looking down over the direction of its flow, is its last village, Duntisborne Abbot's. The centre-piece is the church, which has another saddle-back tower and fine yews cut to the shape of huge chalices. Houses cluster about it and four small roads lead out on to comparatively level ground, in addition to the one coming steeply up from the valley. It was in a warm evening light when I got there, sympathetic to the stonework and the cherry blossom. It was the final thing in this very individual valley and it seemed to me to look the part—the last word in the Duntisborne family of ancient settlements, a full-stop at the end of a poetic sentence.

Branching off on the other side of the Ermine Street, some two miles nearer Gloucester is a byeway leading to Elkstone. Here there is a small church whose Norman work is perhaps the richest of all in the Hills. One of the carvers employed must have been a fellow with an original turn of skill and humour. He has broken the solemn convention of "beak-head" masks in a most unusual fashion. Over the south door this band of ornament takes the form of an array of animals' heads with pointed noses. But one of them is seen to be upside-down. A closer look shows that it is a sub-human being with arms outstretched and hands holding the noses of the masks on either side. Another unusual thing to find is the dovecote over the stone-vaulted chancel. It is quite a roomy place containing many nest-boxes. A newel stair within the chancel gives access to it but the doves' entrance has been glazed and they have been thus debarred. The freshness and completeness of the carved work is due to the Victorian restoration which must have been particularly well done. Anyone who wishes to know what the church looked like in the first part of the last century, with its buckled arches and groggy mouldings, will find an engraving of it in Vol. III of Parker's *Glossary of Architecture*.

Although I stayed a week in Cirencester I was able to see very little of it this time, having to spend all day away from the town, but I was delighted to find that the old market was still being held in booths in the middle of the open street before the church. Of the large churches in the Cotswolds this is the finest. Its enormous porch, in three storeys, has recently been cleaned and now shows an almost dazzling buff against the well-toned grey of the rest of the building. Its interest outweighs its freakishness, but the church would certainly look handsomer without it. Its *raison d'être* still remains a mystery though there seems to be no reasonable doubt that it was made as a hall for one or more of the craft guilds which had their chapels within the church. It has its own wine-cellar and kitchen and a final touch of the secular is given by its oriel windows. Except that one gains access to the church from its vestibule, it is in no sense a 'porch'.

My bicycle was now in the north-east quarter of the Hills, but to get there I had first of all to go north-west into Cheltenham and make a careful calculation about how to get back in the reverse zig-zag. Cheltenham is, in fact, the only place that can be called a "centre" for travel on public transport in the Cotswolds and it has the virtue of producing the best local timetable (showing both rail and bus) of any place I know. It is quite a distinctive production and covers everything except the services of certain local bus proprietors who cannot be induced to issue timetables of any kind. Cheltenham, moreover, is the most admirable place in which to be stranded between buses. Of all towns and spas I have visited it is the most really like a "garden city". It has somehow managed to solve the problem of *rus in urbe* most successfully and, by contrast with the all-stone villages of the surrounding country, its stuccoed frontages in the neo-Grecian convention seem gay.

With these hazards of travel, which took up most of the morning, I reached the Upper Windrush. Limitations of time prevented me going nearer to its source than Guiting Power where, although a small stream, it already has that green, dreamy look that it wears at Minster Lovell and Witney. But hereabouts it appears to have had a different name—the Guiting—lost long since, but still preserved in the villages Guiting Power and Temple Guiting (the diphthong is pronounced as in *guide*, not *guitar*). It is another instance of the local tendency to name places from rivers. Although the valley is deep here it is roomy and the village spreads itself in a pleasant open manner. But the Windrush then passes into a defile which is almost as confined as a gorge, and Naunton is so deep sunk between opposing slopes that it has been obliged to grow up in one long street beside the river. A still greater contrast is seen at the next village, where the river has emerged on to a wide upland plateau. Here, at Bourton-on-the-Water, the striking feature is the way the place divides itself, giving the river so much elbow-room, the houses standing back on either side, to allow it to wander through a wide expanse of lawn-like grass much bigger than an ordinary village green.

Between the Upper Windrush and the bastion-like hill occupied by Stow-on-the-Wold lie the valleys of two tributary streams, the Eye and the Dikler, each of them watering a pair of places with strange names—the Slaughters and the Swells. These streams run with sparkling clear water and join the more obscure and dreamy Windrush below Bourton. The Slaughters are an attractive pair and must be much visited in the summer months, but I found them wonderfully unspoilt. The name is identical with the old English *slough*, a marshy place. It is not so easy to guess why the Swells were so called. Lower Swell lies at the foot of the fine sweep of parkland that clothes the western slope of Stow Hill and is crowned by the sturdy tower of Stow Church. The village has some excellent modern building in houses and walls made of the genuine Cotswold materials. The church has a Saxon sundial and an unusual Norman tympanum over the south door, in which the design of a dove and Tree of Life is cut on the face of several stones fitted together instead of on a single slab.

Upper Swell is at the head of the valley and almost out on the open wolds. Its little church and manor-house stand on the edge of a steep bank, below which the clear Dikler brook runs. A very rural lane goes north from here beside the stream. It looked most inviting to follow and I was torn between this allurement and a desire to revisit the series of long barrows at Pole's Wood which lay close by to the south-west. In this excursion I had not managed to see a single one of those landmarks of the first great Cotswold period, and now I was in what is reckoned to have been the most populous centre of that powerful race of the late Stone Age who built the largest sepulchres that have ever been made in these islands. Besides, hereabouts, there is perhaps a better chance than anywhere else of picking up flint arrow-heads on the open field (as you may guess by looking at the hoard amassed by one man—Canon Royce—on show in St. Edward's Hall at Stow-in-the-Wold).

But already the time-factor was beginning to be of some account, and that is quite fatal to making prehistoric contacts, when one must be not only alone on the "very spot" but free to think back, untied to futurity by anything like the catching of a last bus. So I went forward along that attractive little lane beside the Dikler and came suddenly on a quite un-expected vision. The road dipped into a little hollow and, on the left hand, there was a small range of buildings in buff-coloured local stone which appeared to be a flour-mill with a malting-house added, all combined with a private house, greenhouses, and a charming garden. The mill was still being driven by a proper water-wheel powered by the Dikler which was now pent in a mill-pool of the most prodigious size. It stretched far away down the hollow for about a mile. The pool was dotted with small islands bearing a single birch tree apiece, round which a herd of swans and cygnets cruised in family formations watched by ducks and coots, and the water was as blue as the Mediterranean.

The buildings were not, in fact, those of a mill but a brewery. The proprietor kindly showed me over. His grandfather had started the business in 1865 in premises that appeared to be at least a century earlier and it had remained in the family who had, so far, succeeded in resisting all offers to sell out to one of the big companies. It must be one of the very last small concerns still left. The old water-wheel still worked all the machinery except the refrigerator; draught ale was still produced by traditional methods, and the sample I tasted was excellent. The men had the air of friendly family retainers and I felt more than ever that I was spending time in a real bit of old England.

A little to the west of Arkell's Brewery there is a short length of the Roman road, called Rycknild Street, which turned off the Fosse Way at a point near Bourton-on-the-Water and ran direct to join the Watling Street at Wall, passing through the midst of a site destined in a later age to be occupied by Birmingham. Only this short section (which seems to have been kept alive by users of the village of Condicote) and one other, remain to show where it crossed the Cotswolds. It has become a lost heirloom for which the motorist would probably have found more use than the charioteer.

I came down to the Vale of Moreton through Longborough, which is a singularly dignified village, several of the houses showing signs of medieval work. Its church has a large south transept with exceptionally fine windows in the Decorated style. An unnamed knight of the fourteenth century, wearing a coronet on his helmet, lies within and may have caused that work to be done for the good of his soul.

From there I ran down to Moreton-in-the-Marsh where I stabled my steed for the night at the "White Hart". The earliest moment I was able to get back the next day by public transport was three minutes to one o'clock. Yet Cirencester and Moreton are linked by a first-rate stretch of the Fosse Way, the most direct road in the whole of England, and the distance is twenty-three miles. "In-the-Marsh" is a misleading description, for the stranger would think it to be undoubtedly low-lying. Instead of that it stands more than 400 feet above sea-level on a high plateau which links the Cotswolds with the adjoining range of hills on the east. It is a watershed whose springs doubtless made it somewhat fenny in earlier days and a haunt of wildfowl, as suggested by the original form, "in-Henmarsh". The Evenlode rises here and, a little to the north, tributary streams feed Shakespeare's Avon. Thus, the "henmarsh" contributes both to the North Sea and the Atlantic.

In Saxon times Moreton was a royal manor. Edward the Confessor gave it to his new creation, Westminster Abbey, in whose hands it remained until the Dissolution. The connection is still remembered in the county division which is called the Hundred of Westminster. Another link with Edward the Confessor is Stow-on-the-Wold, four miles away, which, until recent times was called Stow St. Edward. Its parish church is dedicated to the King.

Two miles to the east of Moreton is the Four Shire Stone, now represented by an eighteenth-century monument. It has had many predecessors, the first of which was probably prehistoric. The shires which meet at this point are those of Gloucester, Oxford, Worcester, and Warwick. As the traditional boundary of the Cotswold Hills lies along the right bank of the Evenlode Valley to the south and the left bank of the Knee Brook to the north, it can be taken that the Four Shire Stone also marks this parting with the adjoining range, which is a nameless one but so similar in both physical and architectural features that it is generally thought of as "Cotswold country".

From Moreton to Chipping Campden there is a high road and a low road. The former rises to 943 feet in the Five Mile Drive which is a splendid stretch of the Stow-Evesham road, grand in its amplitude, its fine roadside timber, and its command of view. The other is much more lowly in all respects but shorter by at least a mile and has some nice points. It goes first to Batsford, until lately the home of the Freeman-Mitford family who came there when the first Earl of Redesdale acquired the manor of Moreton in the early nineteenth century and could claim those market tolls which had once belonged to his remote predecessors, the Abbots of Westminster. The market was opened by the ringing of the bell which still hangs in the *tolsey* in the market-square. On page 76 there is a note on this and also on the loyal functionary who died in the course of his duties. His dress may be described to add another touch of colour to our picture. A high-crowned hat banded with gold braid, a long dark coat with scarlet facings and gold cuffs, yellow waistcoat, plush knee-breeches, lemon-coloured stockings, and black brogues.

For more than a mile an avenue of oak trees extends along the level road between Moreton and Batsford. But should it be called an avenue?—for it lacks the formal character of such a plantation. It grows more like hedgerow timber which has been left alone and has a natural charm, lacking in avenues.

Another point about the lower road is that by it you approach Chipping Campden through one of its hamlets, Broad Campden, which presents a sort of visual overture of the town; its houses, cottages and gardens are a foretaste of that pride of maintenance in harmony with the past for which Campden has become famous all over the world. I used to think that in this matter Chipping Campden was a little over self-conscious. On re-visiting it, I relent! In 1900 it was a thoroughly decayed place. It had long lost its importance as a centre of the great woollen industry (out of which it had been created). An attempt to renew its vitality at the end of the eighteenth century by the introduction of silk-throwing to supply the new power-looms at Coventry failed when French silks came into the country duty-free some seventy years later. It dwindled on until 1902, when the Guild of Handicrafts moved from their quarters in East London into an old silk-mill in Sheep Street. This acted as a double stimulant. It gave local employment and it attracted visitors. The place was seen to be one of the least spoiled in all England. Then it began to attract residents who could spend money on repairs and not only its old buildings were restored but also an honest pride in itself. It has now become a chief objective in the tourist industry, but its natural worth and dignity has saved it from the snares which often accompany such fame.

Leaving Campden by the long pull up Dyers' Hill I came to the crest of the escarpment where, through gaps in the thick screen of trees, there are wonderful views over the Vale of Evesham. It was the last day I was to have on my own wheels, the morrow being promised to a friend who had kindly offered to give me a refresher course in South Cotswold by car. The day was getting on and I had to decide how many of the villages at the foot of the escarpment I could see, and which I should begin with. From this point I could reach with equal ease Weston Sub-Edge, Saintsbury, or Willersley. They were all new to me and I wanted to see them. Weston was the farthest from my destination. I should feel bound to visit the other two *en passant*. Willersley was nearest home and to go there straight was the sensible thing to do and would lead me out of temptation.

But Weston Sub-Edge was such a lovely name! Besides, I would pass Dover's Hill on the way, and this was the site of a much earlier and even more remarkable renaissance for Chipping Campden than that produced by the Guild of Handicrafts. Robert Dover, a local attorney, conceived the idea of reviving old English sports in a great festival at Whitsuntide. He appears to have been a very rich man, able to capitalize his idea and offer a large number of prizes to successful competitors. The inaugural event took place in the second year of James I's reign on the small plateau still called Dover's Hill. The promoter had a friend at court who had actually begged a suit of clothes, complete with ruff, from the King. Attired in this he rode on to the ground to open what he called (with the usual classical slant) "The Olympick Cotswold Games". The thing was a huge success, destined to become an annual event which was repeated until 1851 with an inevitable break during the anti-fun regime of the Commonwealth. Ben Jonson and Michael Drayton wrote verses in high praise of it and it is very unlikely that Shakespeare when he retired to Stratford (only twelve miles away) would miss a sight of it. It was exceedingly popular with all classes, "the nobility and gentry" turning out in great force until the first railway trains brought rowdies from the industrial towns. Then it died of the same maltreatment as did the great Shrewsbury Show at about the same time.

After gazing somewhat wistfully at the little old wooden signpost which said "To Dover's Hill" (and had, perhaps, been saying so since the last days of the Olympick Games) I took the middle course and made for Saintsbury with both brakes fully on. The village is situated quite high up above the valley floor with the road going steeply down past it, a site where no modern prospector with all his mechanical advantages would choose

44

to found a settlement. Perhaps an early saint, notoriously insensitive to amenities, chose to fix his shrine at that awkward spot (which seems to be implied in the name) and subsequent parishioners have loyally made the best of it. Maybe it has a still earlier origin, for it lies on the last lap of the pre-Roman Buckle Street which crossed the Hills from this point into the Windrush Valley. But the artist can't complain. For him, the saint chose very well. Some fine trees stand about the place and already we are among orchards, before ever touching bottom in the Vale of Evesham.

The church, though modest in size, is an interesting building of real charm. With its well-proportioned steeple in the Decorated style it seems to have been almost entirely rebuilt during the wool-boom years of the fourteenth century, though two Norman doors have been left. It has managed to keep some of its original glass and benches with carved tracery ends. I was surprised to see the door to the tower stairs hanging by a mere relic of one rusty hinge. The stairs were not of the usual corkscrew type but mounted straight up in the thickness of the wall, as in some castles. The steps were covered with sticks. I crunched up them to the floor of the first stage, then up a tall ladder so that I could put my head into the bell-chamber. The bells, too, were covered with sticks from nesting litter. Evidently this told a sad tale of lack of funds. What an irony! Here was a lovely and unusual Cotswold village with everything that the antiquary, the artist, or the camera-snapper could wish for. Yet its perfect little church was starved for funds while one of the wealthiest streams of tourism rolled in and out of the less admirable Broadway near by.

On the floor of the valley a good level highway follows the configuration of the escarpment like a strategic road along a coast-line. It is a coast-line in reverse, for wherever the cliff is notched by a spring of water a village has grown up and a feeder-lane branches off from the strategic road into it. These natural alcoves are sheltered and well wooded and are the most beautiful and striking feature of the long precipitous eastern fringe of the Cotswolds. The villages are consistently of Cotswold type and well built. Their people, who have had a share in the rich alluvium of the Vale as well as the wold pasture, have been able to make the best of two worlds.

Just here, Worcestershire takes its bite of the Cotswolds. It makes a deep indent following the crest on either side of the valley cut out by the little stream on which Broadway stands, takes in the summit of Middle Hill, the second highest point in the Cotswolds, 1,048 ft., (Cleeve Common over Cheltenham is superior by only 22 ft.) and flattens itself out along what used to be the line of Roman Rycknild Street.

It was late afternoon when I reached Buckland which is set among splendid elms in its alcove under the hill. The young foliage of the trees and the native stone of the village were all bathed in a warm golden glow and I felt that of all the places I had visited this one was going to leave the deepest impression on memory. Its cottages, its manor-house, its church (containing the Buckland mazar bowl, and so much else to enjoy, all beautifully kept), its parsonage with its medieval hall and minstrels' gallery still in use, all steeped in that magical light, seemed like treasure trove, certain to form one of the enrichments of retrospect.

Next, a flying visit to Stanton, but no time for Stanway or the scanty remnants of the great Cistercian Abbey at Hailes, for I wanted to reach Winchcomb to have a peep into the room over the church porch where, I had heard, that enthusiastic local historian, Miss Eleanor Adlard, had arranged a museum. Yet when I got there I thought it too late to trouble the custodian. But the parish church was still open and its principal treasure which is kept in a curtained glass case in the north aisle was accessible, though the light was not very good to see it by. This was a fourteenth-century cope whose orphreys had been cut out by Queen Catherine of Aragon and made up into an altar-cloth. The work was done when the Queen stayed at Sudeley Castle which lies just a mile outside the town. It was still in use until 1872.

By a curious turn of events Sudeley Castle was associated with Henry VIII's last wife as well as his first. The King died in January 1547, and very soon afterwards his young successor presented Sudeley Castle to his uncle, Thomas Seymour (a brother of Henry's third wife), who was then raised to the peerage as Baron Seymour of Sudeley. He had also been granted the principal buildings of the great Benedictine monastery of Winchcomb which he demolished so completely that no trace remains. Not content with these gifts and honours, he made a proposal of marriage

46

to the Princess Elizabeth which was rejected. He was more successful with her step-mother and guardian, the Queen dowager, Catherine Parr, whom he married secretly. Thus, the second Queen Catherine came to live near Winchcomb with her two wards, Princess Elizabeth and Lady Jane Grey.

This was the last point in my point-to-point tour. I intended to consign my bicycle home "per goods" from here and take a train due to leave for Cheltenham in ten minutes. I hurried to the station a mile away and found the platforms deserted, the booking office locked up, and the home signal set at danger. The departure time came and went. By an act of faith I remained some fifteen minutes longer and was duly rewarded. The guard firmly rebutted my statement that he was a quarter of an hour late, pointing out that work was being done on the permanent way and an extra quarter of an hour was allowed. "By the working-timetable", he said, "I am exactly on time." Timetables issued to the public were no concern of his. He offered to sell me a ticket, so I left my bicycle unsecured on the platform to await the station-master's pleasure until he should receive instructions from me, and got in.

My hoped-for bus connection at Cheltenham had gone and I had rather more than an hour to wait for the next. The last red glow of sunset was in the sky and I heard the bells of the parish church at ringing practice. What with all the neo-Grecian panoply of the place the old parish church does not get its fair share of publicity. Yet it is quite in the first rank of the Cotswold churches, and should attract attention if only on account of its Transitional Norman tower which has a fine exterior and, within doors, has one of its capitals carved with a remarkable and enigmatic representation of the *Fall in Eden*. Also, its wheel window in the north aisle, inserted in the wool-gathering fourteenth century, is of cathedral size and unique in a parish church. Guided by the sound and the sunset, I found the little door leading to the tower stairs and groped my way up to the ringing-chamber. The captain of the ringers greeted me with a friendly nod. So I sat awhile harking back over my Cotswold journey, all the glamour of it, down to that golden moment at Buckland, reviving to that perfect accompaniment of the bells. "A real bit of old England still left!" I thought again, set to old English music.

47

# Tetbury

Tetbury stands boldly on a sharp promontory of the Cotswolds at the head of the Avon which trickles down a ravine between the town and railway station, placing them respectively in Gloucestershire and Wiltshire. So steep is the approach on one side that the street is interrupted by three flights of steps. In the centre of the town is a large market-house standing on an open colonnade of stout Doric columns. Like a great many of the old houses in the town it was probably built in the second half of the seventeenth century.

The picture shows the parish church which stands on the highest point. Its body, an early attempt at Gothic revival, is by Francis Hiorne of Warwick and replaces the old nave and chancel which were pulled down in 1777. The side aisles are closed passages with doors numbered like hotel bedrooms, each door giving access to three pews, each pew with a separate door of its own into the middle aisle. It was illuminated by three splendid thirty-six branch chandeliers which still carry their full complement of candles and are lit on feast days.

# Duntisborne Rouse

The Duntisborne (sweetened by local usage into *Dun'sbourne*) is a small stream contributing to the Churn at Cirencester. It occupies one of the most charming little valleys in the Cotswolds and gives its name to four successive places – Duntisborne Rouse, Middle Duntisborne, Duntisborne Leer, and Abbot's Duntisborne. Duntisborne Rouse is said to contain only forty souls, but if they were all to attend divine service in their parish church they would surely fill it. The tiny building is tucked away on a steep slope behind a large Georgian rectory and, for its size, is crammed with interesting features, not the least of which is a crypt with a deeply splayed Norman window, an aumbry, and piscina (now concealed under plaster). A spiral stair leads down to it from the chancel. Its churchyard cross is also remarkable in having escaped the attentions of the iconoclasts.

# Cirencester

The place was built on the ruins of Roman Corinium, a town which was established in the early days of the occupation on the line of the Fosse Way, the frontier of the first part of Britain consolidated by conquest. It became, after London, the biggest junction of the Roman network of roads, and to this fact it owes its prosperity as a merchanting centre in the Middle Ages, a reflection of which is clearly seen in its large and splendidly appointed parish church. Of post-Reformation times it is the houses which speak and there are many interesting ones, ranging from the sixteenth century downwards. The picture shows Coxwell Street with the house called the Woolgatherer's House standing on the right-hand side.

# Coln Rogers

Coln Rogers and its up-stream neighbour, Coln St. Dennis, are a charming couple. Each lies compactly round its interesting little·church in the valley bottom near the river. That at Coln St. Dennis is full of riddles for the antiquary, but that at Coln Rogers has a nave that is plainly Saxon at all four corners with the tell-tale 'long-and-short work' in the quoins, and the unmistakable design of the sundial on the south side which has taken note of changing times for at least a thousand years.

The picture shows one of the roads leading down from the Roman Fosse Way into the village. By another entrance I noted a barn which I reckoned must stand nearly forty feet, from the roadside to the top of its gable. Taking a peep inside I read on a stone 'W. Midweinter 1794' with a primitive representation of corn-in-the-ear. I don't know whether this man was the founder of the barn or not but the name was locally historic, the Midwinters being one of the richest and most powerful families in the days of the Cotswold wool-staplers.

# Bibury

This is an exceedingly picturesque village in the Valley of the Coln. It lies either side of a hollow which has a broad flat bottom of open meadow lying between a rapid mill-stream and a broad placid reach of the Coln which catches reflection where the river makes a turn under a cliff-like escarpment with a screen of tall elms at its foot. Bibury, proper, is on the left bank with the parish church which has remains of Saxon work, including the carved imposts of the chancel-arch. The other half of the village on the right bank is called Arlington. The old houses in the picture link the two communities across the bottom of the water-meadow with the elms and escarpment at their back. They are called Arlington Row and date from the early seventeenth century. They now belong to the National Trust. Their original tenants were engaged in the woollen industry, cloth being tentered on racks on the island meadow opposite their front doors, still called Racks Eye.

# Fairford

This lies where the Coln emerges from its course through the hills into the wide levels of the Upper Thames Valley, broadening as it flows through the long lawn of Fairford Park, and then tumbling over a weir by the old Mill, to flow past the church where seen in the picture. Something has been said (p. 56) about the individuality of the valley from which the river has just emerged and the sustained note of harmony struck at every turn between villages, hamlets, and houses, and the natural setting. This church could not have been more poetically placed to give the final touch. As a work of medieval art it is perhaps the most complete thing we possess with its full range of stained glass, carved stalls and screens, the painted figures of saints and angels on the walls (faint indeed but discernible), and the brass effigy of the man who rebuilt it as it stands in the last decade of the fifteenth century. The river is famous for its trout-fishing, well preserved below the town.

# Northleach

This town was regarded as the premier business centre of the Cotswolds when the wool trade was at its height in the fourteenth and fifteenth centuries. In its large church the memorial brasses which still remain are chiefly to woolmen and woolstaplers whose feet rest on the woolsack and (in one instance) on the back of a Cotswold sheep. Both this church and that of the rival town of Chipping Campden had their naves rebuilt fairly late in the fifteenth century and the arcades are of identical design, having octagonal piers whose sides are treated with a hollow chamfer, with capitals to match and flattened arches above, giving an un-English look and slightly oriental touch to the buildings and making them seem more bare and empty than the normal Gothic treatment. But with their old stained glass and medieval colouring the effect would doubtless have been far different. The south porch at Northleach, however, is an individual achievement which for beauty of design could hardly be beaten by that of any other parish church in the kingdom. Compared with Chipping Campden, the old town is much shrunk and deteriorated, but since the '39–'45 War it has been augmented by a large number of Council houses on the side remote from that shown in the picture. The addition interferes re-markably little with the look of the place, and the grafting of a young and vigorous community on to this ancient and honourable but palpably withering stock could be good for both.

# Burford

This ancient town which was one of the first to achieve self-government after the Norman Conquest lies in the lower Valley of the Windrush, where some of the best building stone is got. It has managed to preserve a collection of old houses even more representative of changes in style and manners over five centuries than Chipping Campden. Its large church with a central Norman tower is full of interest and exceptional in plan. It figured in one dramatic episode in English history when a regiment of the Roundhead army mutinied in Salisbury four months after the death of Charles I. The men intended to join another disaffected force at Banbury and were on the march in that direction when Fairfax closed in on them at Burford, and Cromwell also appeared on the scene. The mutineers were overpowered and shut up in the church for four days, after which, three of them were shot in the churchyard. This was the last affair in which Fairfax acted as Commander-in-Chief of the Army. It crushed an early manifestation of communism called the Leveller Movement. And one of those Levellers put his stay in the church on permanent record by cutting his name on the lead lining of the font – 'Anthony Sedley 1649 prisner'. For those interested in old buildings and local idiom the place is a rich store and Mrs Gretton's *Burford Past and Present* is the key to unlock it.

# Minster Lovell

The village lies in the lower Windrush Valley and is mainly built along a single street on the left bank of the river. The name is associated with the Lovell family, who owned the manor from the twelfth to the last quarter of the fifteenth century, when it was lost through backing the wrong side in the final struggle of the Wars of the Roses. The last holder was Francis, Lord Lovell, a Yorkist and strong supporter of Richard III. He is still remembered in most history books from that couplet coined by a political opponent:

> *The Cat, the Rat, and Lovell our Dog*
> *Rule all England under a Hog.\**

It was Lord William, the father of Francis, who built the fine church and whose effigy in alabaster lies there with the Yorkist chain of suns round his neck. He also rebuilt the adjoining Manor-house whose ruin is now cared for by the Ministry of Works.

The half-timbered building shown in the picture (a rare type of construction in the Cotswolds) and now part of a hotel, is said to date from 1490 – three years after the Battle of Stoke, when 'our Dog', fighting for the pretender Lambert Simnel, was defeated and mysteriously disappeared.

* It will be remembered that the Rat was Sir Richard Ratcliffe and the Cat, Sir William Catesby, both favourites of Richard III. The home of the Catesbys was not far away, at Chastleton, near Moreton-in-the-Marsh. Chastleton House was built in Elizabethan times on the site of their old manor-house and their tombs are in the church close by.

# Naunton

This lies deep in the heart of the Wolds, in the upper Valley of the Windrush. The farm lands fall steeply down on either side, but the village follows the river with a single level street. Confinement of room has not favoured the usual post-war expansion. The place remains detached and mellow. There is a fine four-square dovecote (gabled on all sides) with stone nesting boxes said to number nearly two thousand, an amenity lost on the hens which now live there. A house which has the look of one built by a Jacobean yeoman is pointed out as 'Cromwell's House' because he is said to have slept there and the very bedroom is remembered. The story no doubt recalls an incident after Edge Hill or the fight at Stow even if they haven't got the name of the distinguished stranger right. It must have been near that time that the church was so heavily doctored as to make it one of the plainest in the district. But its well-carved medieval stone pulpit has remained untouched.

# Bourton-on-the-Water

This place has become very attractive to tourists. It is not like anywhere else in or out of the Cotswolds. Its wide open space with trees and ample green lawns, and the dreamy Windrush winding through the midst under many bridges of unusual design (like that in the picture which has no parapet); its church in the background which has an extra-Gothic Victorian nave joined to a Hanoverian tower with cupola and bull's-eye windows, give one the feeling of being in an exhibition and not an English village. Even the solid stone houses which stand around look as if they had had their dates and sizes appropriately mixed to heighten the illusion. And there is another thing! It came into the head of a local innkeeper to make a model of the village, one-ninth natural size, a work taking six men four years. You can see it by dropping a coin into a turnstile. When you examine these miniature replicas of the buildings you saw outside and come to the inn itself, there, sure enough, in the back premises, is the model of the model. This has an odd effect for, when you re-emerge and look again on that slightly unearthly scene, you appear to be gazing at the model of a model of a model.

# Lower Slaughter

The two villages bearing this curious name seem to have gained it not from a scene of bloodshed but a slough. Yet the little Eye brook, which goes through their midst, so far from being muddy is one of the clearest and most sparkling of the Cotswold streams. On entering Lower Slaughter it turns the wheel of a mill which is still in active service (a happy overture, rare these days) and passes on to grace the double village street in the manner shown in the picture.

Upper Slaughter, though only a mile away is a village entirely different in character. Its post-office is one of the hardest to find without local direction, being inconspicuously located within a small quadrangle of houses. Its church contains some fine bits of Norman work, but all re-arranged confusingly in two several reconstructions of the fifteenth and nineteenth centuries. It has one of the finest Cotswold manor-houses, a four-square Elizabethan house of twelve gables built on a stone-vaulted medieval undercroft. Both places are situated in (and must take their name from) the Hundred of Slaughter, an old civil division of Gloucestershire, so that the 'slough' alluded to was marshy ground elsewhere than by these villages.

# Stow-on-the-Wold

Six main roads meet here at an immense market-square which stretches far behind the spot on which the photographer stood to take his picture of the cross – it was perhaps moved from a central place when the ancient shaft was given a new head in 1876. The square was the site of a biannual fair that was famous in the great days of the Cotswold wool trade, and it is said that at one of these gatherings 20,000 sheep were sold. Even the erection of a large Victorian assembly hall and other buildings has left enough room for a battalion parade-ground. The church, too, is large and its broad tower is just what the steeple of a hilltop town should be. The drovers bringing in their flocks to the great fair along those several roads would see it from far away.

The Battle of Stow was the last fight in the Civil War (at least during the life of the King). It took place a mile to the north of the town in the spring of 1646, shortly after King Charles's cause had been ruined at Naseby and by the collapse of his army in the West Country. Here old Sir Jacob Astley, last of the King's generals, was heavily defeated. Visitors to the town who are interested in this period will find in the hall (above-mentioned) a unique collection of portraits, many of them original, of Caroline and Cromwellian notables – including Mrs Cromwell – armour, and other relics from the bequest of an enthusiastic collector. Canon Royce's fine collection of flint arrow-heads and other local prehistoric finds mentioned on page 40 is also in this interesting but somewhat neglected museum.

# Upper Swell

The picture shows the manor-house (now a farm) which stands only a few yards from the church, both situated on a steep brow overlooking the little River Dikler which here forms a large pool, probably first contrived as a manorial fishpond. The upper room with the big mullioned window has a fine moulded plaster ceiling and cornice in Jacobean style and also an immense stone fireplace with projecting hood. The iron fireback is dated 1610, which probably speaks for the whole house except part of the kitchen where a pointed doorway suggests a link with an earlier house. At the back of the house an upstairs window has 'Cheese Room' marked above it, a reminder that it claimed exemption from the window-tax (imposed between 1695 and 1851).

The near neighbourhood is wonderfully rich in antiquarian interest. On the high ground between Upper and Lower Swell several long barrows mark the resting places of notable Stone Agers who colonized the Cotswolds in great force. Here, they are in a group placed closer together than elsewhere. Between Upper Swell and Condicote is an earthwork fort of the early Celtic immigrants, and the line of the Roman Road called Rycknild Street runs north, passing a little to the west of the village. Numerous coins, bits of pottery, and other relics of the 'occupying power' have been unearthed in the parish.

# Moreton-in-the-Marsh*

The picture shows the market square which lies athwart the Roman Fosse Way. The old market toll-house called the *tolsey* with its clock and bell is seen on the right. The bell, dated 1663, was rung not only as a signal for the market to open but also at 5 o'clock every morning and at curfew. This ancient marking of time went on until 1862, when the last manorial official, who was market-keeper, parish constable, church beadle, and town-crier, met his death trying to put a drunken man into his lock-up in the basement of the tolsey. The building on the left in the form of a market-house is the Memorial Hall built in 1887 by the Mitford family in memory of the first Earl of Redesdale, the lord of the manor. The building with the tall flagpole is the older part of the White Hart Hotel where a room is still shown in which Charles I slept on his way from Oxford to Evesham in 1643.

* The abbreviation to 'Moreton-in-Marsh' recently adopted seems to have been based on the now discredited derivation of 'Marsh' from 'March', a boundary. Such dismemberment spoils the euphony of a good name and destroys its proper complemental relationship with its neighbours, Barton-on-the-Heath and Stow-on-the-Wold.

# Chipping Campden

This town was once the rival of Northleach as a centre of the Cotswold wool trade. It then took second place. But it has been far more successful than the other in preserving its old buildings, and its present fame rests on that. Its long main street is composed of houses dating from the fourteenth to the eighteenth century with only rare interruption by anything more recent. The dominant style is that of the seventeenth century, at which time there lived the town's most important benefactor, the first Viscount Campden, a London mercer, still referred to locally by the first honour he gained – Sir Baptist Hicks. Among his public works were the market-house and the row of almshouses seen in the picture. The huge mansion which he built was garrisoned for the King during the Civil War but set on fire by the royalist commander when he withdrew his forces on the rather silly pretext that it might be of use to the enemy. The stone cupolas of the gateway (seen on the right) are among the few survivals of that great place. The nave of the church (late fifteenth century) closely resembles that of Northleach, but the tower design shows a peculiar and not very graceful departure from normal practice by having pairs of buttresses united at parapet level by four-centred arches mounting pinnacles.

# North Cotswold

A long view from Fish Hill, on the edge of the western escarpment, above Broadway overlooking the Vale of Evesham. If Kent had not thought of the name 'The Garden of England' first, it might well have been adopted by this wide valley through which Shakespeare's Avon flows from Stratford to join the Severn at Tewkesbury. It has indeed much in common with Kent, being a land both of orchards and hop-gardens. And the orchards begin as soon as you cross the hills and begin the descent. In the Middle Ages the Vale must have been as rich in vineyards, for along the river and close under the hills stood five of the largest Benedictine monasteries in England – Evesham, Pershore, Tewkesbury, Gloucester, and Winchcomb and, in addition, the Cistercian house of Hailes. Another narcotic crop beside the grape also flourished exceedingly near Winchcomb in the seventeenth century. That was tobacco. But our colonists in Virginia persuaded the Government to forbid its cultivation. There was much local opposition to this and it was only eradicated by ploughmen being sent under escort of troops to tear the farmers' crops from the soil.

# Stanton

This village lies in a short re-entrant valley in the western escarpment of the Cotswolds, under Shun-barrow Hill, one of the highest points in the range, lacking only four feet to make the round thousand, and crowned by a prehistoric earthwork where finds have been made dating back to the Bronze Age. The two byeways leading into the village from the main road are flanked by splendid avenues of elm, oak, and chestnut. The place contains some fine and interesting old houses, some with lovely gardens. Warren House (built when the Warren family moved down to this more genial spot from Snowshill on the high ground above) is dated 1577 and has been linked with the name of Catherine Parr, the last of Henry VIII's wives. It is true that Henry presented her with the manor of Stanton of which he had relieved Winchcomb Abbey after the Dissolution of the Monasteries but that would seem to be the only connection. Queen Catherine died at the home of her second husband, Lord Seymour of Sudeley, at Sudeley Castle which is only a few miles away. Her tomb in the parish church there was desecrated and rifled in the eighteenth century. The picture shows the ancient village cross at Stanton capped with its post-Reformation head.

# Cheltenham

The picture shows the Promenade, the most striking and interesting feature in the Georgian layout of the Spa. At the beginning of the last century the site was a brickfield through which the little River Chelt trickled. The buildings were begun and the avenues planted in the year 1818, the latter being aligned so that the pump-room of the Imperial Spa should close the vista, a building replaced twenty years later by the much more imposing Queen's Hotel (restored and modernized, 1957) designed by R. W. Jearrad who was responsible for the planning and development of the Lansdowne estate. The idea of giving a number of separate dwelling-houses a single architectural unity had been developed by the Woods in their works at Bath and was continued by the Cheltenham builders, as is well seen in the picture. Across the broad thoroughfare and its now well-grown avenue are most of the best shops in the town. The statue is that of Dr E. A. Wilson, a Cheltenham man, who was Chief of the Scientific Staff of the British Antarctic Expedition of 1910–13. He died with Captain Scott on the Great Ice Barrier. He was a fine artist as well as a doctor and zoologist and his water-colour sketches of the South Polar region have been collected and preserved at the Scott Polar Research Institute at Cambridge.

# Hard Weather

This wintry scene is near Shepscombe, a village in a valley near Painswick. On the heights above, conditions are generally very much worse than appear in the picture. One writer in the early nineteenth century says: 'The unsheltered state of the Cotswolds exposes them to the unmitigated effects of cold winds, and consequently throughout their whole extent a sharp climate predominates.' But the native Cotswold sheep which was such a valuable source of national income in the Middle Ages kept herself warm in a fleece weighing on the average fourteen pounds – she still does, but her numbers are reduced to one last pedigree flock. The word 'sheep' occurs naturally in many connections in the Cotswolds, and more than one town has a 'Sheep Street', so that one might think that Shepscombe was a combe so called because sheep were brought down from the higher ground to winter there. But the writer above quoted spells it 'Shepscom', while in the earliest records it is 'Sebbescumbe'; so we are left guessing.

# Mid-Cotswold

The picture shows a farmer in the neighbourhood of Painswick drilling winter wheat in the fall of the year. One of the most notable features in the Cotswolds is the manner in which rock, soil, and buildings blend in every landscape. The buildings, both masonry and roofing slabs, come from the native rock, which is of a light golden colour when taken from the quarry, weathering to grey. The soil is a rich golden brown, varying in shade from place to place. When freshly turned by October ploughing, it makes a rich contribution to the splendid show of Autumn colouring, for this is still a land of English hardwood trees in woods and hedgerows – here, so far, the invasion of the economic conifer in regimented plantations has been successfully resisted. On fine November days one may look out from one of the high promontories in the western escarpment and see this glory of the turn of the leaf succeeded by another glory when the sun sets over the Welsh hills and the Severn estuary.

82895

# Frocester Court

The manor of Frocester had belonged to the monks of Gloucester since the time of the Saxon kings. At the end of the thirteenth century the Abbot of Gloucester built a tythe-barn there which exceeded the length of the nave of his church (now the cathedral). This barn is still in perfect condition and regular use. It is the largest tythe-barn in England (inside measurement 184 ft. by 29 ft. 7 in.). In design the huge roof anticipates certain elements which did not come into general use until much later. The thrust is countered by flying-buttresses reminiscent of those in the choir of Gloucester Cathedral. After the dissolution of the Abbey the manor came into the possession of Sir George Huntley, who largely rebuilt the Court in 1554 and gave it its present form. In 1574 he entertained the Queen there on her way to Berkeley Castle – an authentic instance of 'Elizabeth spent the night here', as the parson noted the event in his parish registers. The house does not look its age. Like the great barn, the choice and treatment of its stone is in the best Cotswold tradition.

# Owlpen

This manor-house and small parish church lies at the bottom of a deep pocket-like valley under the heights of Uley and is surrounded by dense woodland. But the name which seems so fitting and romantic does not refer to owls but to the Saxon thegn, Olla, who had his pen, or enclosure, in this charming hollow. The front of the house bears the date 1616 and the initials T.D. for Thomas Daunt. There are several monuments to the family in the church. This was rebuilt in 1828 and in 1875 the previous architect's ideas about Gothic were corrected and put to rights in all except his plaster ceiling to which he had applied a fanciful lierne vault in wood. This remains; a choice sample of Hanoverian Gothic Revival. The small building on the left is the manorial court-house.

# South Cotswold

This picture is taken on the south-west fringe of the Cotswolds, overlooking the large four-aisled church of Almondsbury. The country seen beyond is the Vale of Berkeley, at the entrance to which the River Severn is joined by its sister stream, the Wye, the two then immediately merging their identity in the Bristol Channel. The point where this happens and the estuary suddenly opens out so that one can speak of 'the coast' instead of 'the left bank' is four miles west of Almondsbury. Just there the Severn Tunnel crosses under to carry the railway into Wales, while the car-ferry from Aust to Beachley, near Chepstow, crosses over the water a little way above it. The Wye comes down through a deep gorge between the Monmouth hills and those of the Forest of Dean (which can be seen from this point) and the Romans who worked iron in the Forest must have used a crossing near the present one (there are indications of a settlement near Aust) connecting with their main road which goes through Almondsbury to Gloucester.